KT-453-433

THE LIFE & TIMES OF
MAHATMA GANDHI

THE LIFE & TIMES OF

Mahatma Gandhi

BY
James Brown

This edition first published by Parragon Books

Produced by
Magpie Books Ltd
7 Kensington Church Court
London W8 4SP

Copyright © Parragon Book Service Ltd 1994

Cover picture & illustrations courtesy of: Mary Evans
Picture Library; Rex Features; Associated Press.

ISBN 1 85813 927 9

A copy of the British Library Cataloguing in Publication
Data is available from the British Library.

Typeset by Hewer Text Composition Services, Edinburgh
Printed in Singapore by Printlink International Co.

CHILDHOOD AND MARRIAGE

Mohandas Karamchand Gandhi was born in Porbandar, India, on 2 October 1869. He was the sixth and last child of Karamchand (Kaba) Gandhi by his fourth and last wife, Putlibai. Kaba, like his father before him, served the local Ranas or princelings of Kathiawad.

India then as now was mostly populated by Hindus. But it was bigger, for the modern states of Pakistan and Bangladesh were part of it; their secession would be one of the last set backs of Gandhi's life. It was ruled not by Indians but by the British, whose abandonment of their colony would be one of Gandhi's greatest triumphs.

The Gandhis were Hindus. As such they belonged to a caste, a hereditary social rank. In principle there were four castes which in theory determined the occupations of those born into them. The highest were the Brahmins, who were meant to be priests and scholars; then came the ruling and fighting caste, the Kshatriyas; then the Vaisyas, farmers and traders; and lastly the Sudras, peasants and workers. At the bottom of the heap were the Untouchables, who undertook the jobs that all the other Hindus regarded as impure (often, essential sanitation work) and were outcasts for their pains. The system had become more complicated over time so that hundreds of sub-castes developed. The Gandhis belonged to Modh Bania, a business caste.

Kaba Gandhi decided that Mohandas should succeed him eventually in the service of the princes of Kathiawad (as with much in Indian life, birth could count for more than talent). What exactly persuaded Kaba Gandhi that his youngest son should be so favoured is unclear. Academically he was utterly undistinguished at school. But perhaps that did not weigh much with Gandhi senior whose own formal schooling was slight.

Mohandas got married at the age of thirteen. By the standards of his religion and time this was perfectly normal. His father selected an appropriate bride, Kasturbai, the daughter of a friend in Porbandar. It was to be a triple wedding – his brother Karsandas and a cousin were being married at the same time. The idea was to save money, for Hindu weddings could be ruinously expensive.

The Gandhis were then living at Rajkot, five days' journey away by cart. Gandhi senior was detained by business until three days before the ceremony. He dashed to the wedding by special stage-coaches. On the last day of the journey the coach overturned, and Kaba Gandhi arrived swathed in bandages.

Kaba Gandhi never fully recovered from his coach accident, and his health soon deteriorated. The young Gandhi helped with the nursing. By 1885 Kaba's condition was poor. One night as Gandhi was caring for him, an uncle relieved him. Gandhi went off to inflict his attentions on the already pregnant Kasturbai. A short while later, word came that his father was dying. Gandhi was smitten with guilt. He later wrote:

'It was a blot I have never been able to efface or forget, and I have always thought that, although my devotion to my parents knew no bounds and I would have given up anything for it, yet it was weighed and found unpardonably wanting because my mind was at the same moment in the grip of lust.'

To add to his burden of self-reproach, Kasturbai's baby died soon after birth.

These events changed Gandhi's life in two ways. Suddenly his family was much poorer, and some decision had to be made about his future as the chosen son. At the same time Gandhi personally felt he had gone wrong, and cast about trying to get his moral bearings. Perhaps somewhat surprisingly, his extended family decided to scrape together their resources and send him to England to train as a lawyer. The solution to the other problem, however, was a lifetime's spiritual quest.

ENGLAND

The Gandhi who set off to Bombay *en route* to London was a somewhat unlikely candidate for a cosmopolitan education. He was acutely shy, and the idea of such a journey was unusual not just for him, but for anyone from his background.

His mother was deeply concerned about the move. Eventually she allayed her doubts by following the advice of a family friend: in front of her, she required Mohandas to take a

solemn oath to abstain from wine, women
and meat. His caste was harder to win round.
No one of the Modh Banias had ever made
such a trip. Fearing that ritual purity would
prove impossible to maintain, they solemnly
declared Gandhi an outcast.

Arriving in London, he put up at the
Victoria Hotel. He had letters of introduc-
tion to several Indians resident in England.
One of the most useful of these contacts was
the formidable Dr P.J. Mehta. This gentle-
man called on the gauche Gandhi in formal
dress, with a top hat. While they spoke
Gandhi toyed with the hat, and in his
ignorance brushed it the wrong way, to
the doctor's annoyance. Even so, the doctor
gave him sound advice: to find less expensive
quarters.

Gandhi was in earnest about qualifying as a lawyer, as his family expected him to, and he soon reassessed his high-flown ways. He moved from lodging to lodging for the sake of economy, ending up in a single room, cooking his own meals on a stove in the corner. He also took to walking everywhere, which toughened him up and saved him paying fares.

The vow imposed by his mother made for some difficulties. Gandhi had no personal objection to eating meat, but he did have a deep commitment to keeping his word. At first he found such vegetarian fare as he could get insipid and unsatisfying. His shyness held him back from asking for more, and he was often very hungry. Then he found a vegetarian restaurant in Farringdon. Not only was the food good, but the restaurant also supplied justification for its bill of fare in the shape of Henry Salt's *Plea for Vegetarianism*. Gandhi devoured both food and pamphlet. Here at last was a justification for the position to which he was committed by his vow. As he read, conviction grew upon him. Suddenly, diet was placed in the context of much larger issues: health, morality and self-realization. It was a theme which anticipated the concerns of the later Gandhi, for whom diet was a crucial matter, and something with which he would experiment (often to the dismay of his friends).

Vegetarianism provided Gandhi with the greater part of his social life outside his studies, which he was diligently pursuing at the Inner Temple. He would in due course join the London Vegetarian Society and serve on its committee. But the issue of diet also put him in touch with a larger circle of radical people and ideas. Among these were ideas originating in India. Two theosophists introduced him to Sir Edwin Arnold's translation of the *Bhagavad Gita*. This is a religious text, which forms part of the great Indian epic, the *Mahabharata*. It would become crucial to Gandhi's teaching later on. He was also fascinated by Arnold's own poem based on Buddhist teachings, *The Light of Asia*. Fellow vegetarians persuaded him to reconsider Christianity, of which in India he had been dismissive, having encountered it largely through dogmatic missionaries. But now he read Christ's Sermon on the Mount with interest. The main characteristic of Gandhi as a religious teacher, his readiness to recognize truth in other faiths, without departing from his own Hinduism, was already taking shape. The doubts about

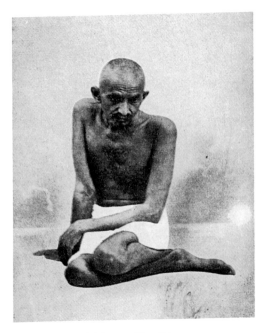

Mahatma Gandhi

Gandhi's birthplace

religion as such to which he had been prey back in India were put behind him.

Gandhi was called to the bar on 10 June 1891. *The Vegetarian* carried a valedictory interview with him. His friends threw a farewell vegetarian party for him, at which he proved almost as tongue-tied and shy as he had been when he arrived. Given that he lacked academic flair and was studying in a language that did not come easily to him, Gandhi had evidently worked ferociously hard during his three years in London. Whether it would do him any good back in India was, however, a moot point.

SOUTH AFRICA

If Gandhi had expected a rapturous home-coming he was sadly mistaken. His brother Laxmidas met him off the boat with the news that their mother was dead. The news had been kept from him so as not to disturb his studies, but now he had to know.

Professional disappointment followed perso-nal grief. Though he was now an English-trained lawyer, that did not necessarily help him much when it came to securing work in

India, and it was vital that he earn a living. Apart from anything else, he had left Kasturbai with their first child, Harilal, when he went to England, and she was soon pregnant again. Eventually an opening came in shape of an offer from a well-to-do merchant. Abdulla Sheth was originally from Porbandar, but now had substantial business interests in South Africa, where he was engaged in a lawsuit with another Indian Muslim trader called Tyeb Sheth. Gandhi was to go to South Africa for a year to assist in this suit for a fee of a hundred guineas.

In May 1893 Gandhi arrived in Durban, leaving Kasturbai at home with their second child, Manilal. Odd as it may seem now, there was little overt racism in the London of his day, so South Africa was Gandhi's first experience of it. He had to travel from

Durban to Pretoria, for which Abdulla gave him a first-class railway ticket. All went well until the train steamed into Pietermaritzburg. A white passenger glanced into Gandhi's compartment and summoned the guard. Gandhi was ejected onto the platform, and the train Gandhi, steamed off. He passed a bitterly cold night contemplating not just his own problem, but the larger problem of which it was a part. After further difficulties, Gandhi finally arrived in Pretoria.

His experiences impelled him to political action. With the help oddly enough of Tyeb Sheth, his employer's opponent in the lawsuit, he started to organize meetings of Indians to campaign against discrimination. He also studied the plight of his fellow-countrymen. They formed a substantial minority, many of whom had been brought over as indentured labourers which effectively made it impossible for them to resign if ill-treated by their employers. A few were in business and some of them prospered. But they were all subject to a sorry round of insults and prejudice. Gandhi would later comment that 'It has always been a mystery to me how men can feel themselves honoured by the humiliation of their fellow-beings', but he was about to have every opportunity to observe this mystery at close quarters.

Meanwhile the lawsuit went ahead. Though Abdulla had initially been somewhat at a loss to know what to do with a lawyer whom his Indian office had hired without properly consulting him, Gandhi proved instrumental in resolving the case, and in a manner typical of himself. First of all he persuaded both parties to submit to arbitration, rather than flog the case through the courts. This went against Tyeb. It could have ruined him. But Gandhi then persuaded Abdulla to accept payment of the damages in instalments. The honour of both parties was preserved.

Once the case was settled, Gandhi prepared to return to India. A farewell party was thrown for him, in the course of which he happened to pick up a newspaper and glance at an article on proposed changes to the Indian franchise. Effectively he realized that the dominant white minority planned to rob Indians of the vote in Natal. In a trice the party changed to a planning meeting for a campaign – and Gandhi was staying to run it.

POLITICAL APPRENTICESHIP

The scope of the political struggle grew. This was for two reasons. On the one hand, the white authorities were intent on passing measures which, directly or indirectly, would institutionalize racism. At the same time, Gandhi's ethical ideals grew beyond the specifically political and civil context of the immediate struggle, to encompass issues relating to religion and to life-style as a whole.

An organization called the Indian National
Congress had been established in India in
1885 and had rapidly acquired prestige as the
forum in which the elite of educated Indians
voiced their opinions. Gandhi knew little of
it beyond the name, but it inspired his Natal
Indian Congress. Unlike the body that
inspired it, the Natal Congress functioned
all the year round, handling press relations,
organizing meetings, and steadily supporting
the cause of Indian rights. Its membership
was also broader. One day a Tamil burst into
Gandhi's office, teeth broken, clothes torn
and bloody, and respectfully plucked off his
headscarf. He was Balasundaram, an indentured labourer, who was being beaten by his
employer. But it was illegal for him simply to
resign and find another job. Gandhi inter-
vened and secured his release. Suddenly he
had captured the imaginations of a whole

Bombay in the 1890s

Nationalists attack British homes

class of poorer Indians who became involved in Congress's work.

In order to reach the community at large, Gandhi went into journalism. In 1903 he launched a weekly: *Indian Opinion*. Initially it was published in four languages: English, Gujarati, Hindi and Tamil. It was also subsidized by Gandhi personally – to the tune of £75 a month. His legal practice was fortunately lucrative, but even so this was a huge sum. His first move was to appeal to the community for support.

A number of Westerners rallied to Gandhi's cause. Among them were a couple of fellow vegetarians. Albert West was a printer who undertook to work on *Indian Opinion*. He found it, from a business point of view, in a bad way. At about the same time, Gandhi met (again through vegetarian connections) a young Jewish lawyer, Henry Polak, who was to become a supporter. Meanwhile Gandhi had to travel to Durban to sort out the newspaper. Just before his departure, Polak lent him a copy of John Ruskin's *Unto This Last*.

Ruskin was a Victorian art and social critic. *Unto This Last* is an attempt to outline where real value lies in the various processes a society engages in: not in inanimate riches but in the variety and vitality of human life. It is a protest against the inhuman effects of industrialization and ruthless individualism, and a plea for the individual worker and his or her craft. Gandhi devoured the book overnight on the train to Durban. It chimed with ideas for social reform which he had already encountered in reading some of the

non-fiction of Leo Tolstoy, the Russian
novelist and social critic.

The immediate effect of reading Ruskin was
that Gandhi got off the Durban train, sleep-
less but elated, and proposed moving the
whole outfit of *Indian Opinion* to a commune
which they could establish on a farm. To the
happily named Phoenix Farm they moved at
the end of 1904. Gandhi's own family was to
spend much time there, as Gandhi progres-
sively repudiated earthly possessions and
pursued the ideal of a self-sufficient, mu-
tually reliant community. When the focus of
his operations moved to Johannesburg he
would establish with the help of a German
sympathizer, Hermann Kallenbach, another
such community which he dubbed Tolstoy
Farm.

Gandhi himself could not spend as much time as he would have liked in these communities, where he could experiment, among other things, with his ideas about health and diet. A succession of racist measures were proposed or actually passed by the white authorities, and Gandhi had to maintain the larger Indian organization that would counter them, occasionally travelling back to London or India to put the Indian case and get help putting pressure on the South African authorities. Those authorities could be slippery to deal with. It was required, for example, that indentured labourers at the expiry of their indentures pay a tax of £25 or leave. This was a prohibitively vast sum for such people. Under pressure this was changed to £3, but it was now payable by every member of the labourer's family – the effect for most of them was pretty much the same. More generally inflammatory was a policy requiring Indians to register and supply a full set of finger-prints – a procedure normally applicable only to criminals. The measure's real intent was to choke off immigration and facilitate deportation.

Gandhi had to find some appropriate weapon with which to resist such measures. He was determined that their action must be disciplined and peaceful. At a mass meeting in a theatre in Johannesburg in 1906, several thousand spontaneously took a solemn oath not to comply with registration.

Gandhi sought to formulate a policy which ideologically owed something to Tolstoy's pacifism, but also related to the Hindu ideal of ahimsa. However, he wanted it to be distinctive. 'Passive resistance' sounded a little weak, so he ran a competition for a new name. His cousin, Maganlal, scooped the prize with 'satyagraha', meaning strength in truth, or soul force. It was a term that would ring throughout the rest of Gandhi's career. It involved non-violent resistance and a disciplined readiness to suffer for the sake of a specific grievance. The ultimate object was not to defeat one's opponent, but to make him reconsider his position, and so finally convert him. As Gandhi came to expound it, these lofty principles should not preclude a readiness to compromise on inessential issues in order to secure the main point.

As the struggle escalated, Gandhi saw the inside of a prison for the first time – and found it a useful time to read and gather his

On the Salt Tax pilgrimage

A Calcutta street in 1930

strength for renewed activity. In all, he was to spend a total of six years in gaol by the end of his life. He also showed more and more flair for devising impressive protests. When General Smuts went back on the deal Gandhi thought he had struck with him, Gandhi arranged a solemn burning of thousands of registration certificates in the grounds of a Johannesburg mosque. The authorities also helped by playing into his hands. For example, in 1913 a ruling of the Supreme Court made Hindu, Muslim and Parsee marriages legally invalid, thus in effect turning respectable and devout wives into concubines in the eyes of the law. Its accidental effect was to drive women to join the struggle as well, which anticipated the later involvement of women in Gandhi's style of nationalist politics back in India.

The women marched off into the Natal mining district, where outraged Indian miners downed tools. The owners were already in dispute with their white workers and were alarmed at the prospect of the Indians striking as well. In response to the action of the authorities, the strike spread. Gandhi now had industrial workers involved in the struggle as well as women. He gathered his supporters together in a huge pilgrimage, which, in accordance with satyagraha, ended up in crammed prison cells. Even so the protest spread, and the authorities overplayed their hand. International pressure from the Viceroy of India and the British Government was also being brought to bear on the South African authorities. At this point, fate gave Gandhi the chance for his master-stroke. He had organized another march for January 1914, but at this point the white railway-workers went on strike. To another man this would have been an opportunity to strike while one's foe was beleaguered. But such was not the way of satyagraha; sooner than exploit his opponents' plight, Gandhi cancelled the march, and scored a tremendous, internationally recognized moral victory. At last, Smuts agreed to negotiate in earnest. The main demands were met: the £3 tax was abolished, the indenture system was to be run down, residence regulations were eased, and marriages were officially recognized.

HOME COMING

Gandhi had been trying to get back to India for some time. In 1901 he had left South Africa and had become involved in Indian politics. But, before leaving, he had given a promise that if his South African friends needed his services within the year, he would return. They had duly summoned him and he went.

Gandhi's view of the British Empire and his position in the spectrum of Indian politics had changed since then. In the course of his South African struggles he had found himself in London in 1909. He reassessed his opinion of Western civilization radically:

'Looking at this land, I at any rate have grown disillusioned with Western civilization. The people whom you meet on the way seem half-crazy. They spend their days in luxury or in making a bare living and retire at night thoroughly exhausted. In this state of affairs, I cannot understand when they can devote themselves to prayers.'

The immediate upshot of this was a book called *Hind Swaraj* ('Indian Home Rule') in which Gandhi set forth a programme of political change in India aimed not just at putting Indians in the positions of power then occupied by the British, but at recovering and reinventing the true Indian culture and national identity. What he proposed was not merely self-government of a narrowly political kind, but self-realization in a broader cultural and religious sense. That breadth of vision would be characteristic of Gandhi's work for the remainder of his life.

Gandhi's work in Africa had been followed with interest in India, and had brought him to the notice of prominent Indian politicians, in particular Gopal Krishna Gokhale. Gokhale was a Congress leader of considerable prestige. He had gone to Africa to support Gandhi's campaign, and at the same time was concerned to find some role for Gandhi's formidable talents back in India. It was to meet Gokhale that in July of 1914 Gandhi sailed not straight to India, but to England.

Gokhale took stock of Gandhi's radical views. It was not easy to see exactly how he was going to fit into Congress's kind of politics, which at that time was mostly an affair of an educated Indian elite. Gokhale himself was on the moderate, constitutional wing of Congress, unlike his rival, the more fiery B.G. Tilak. Both these figures had something to offer Gandhi by way of practical support and example. In 1905 Gokhale had founded a society called the Servants of India, who were committed to the ideal of political and social service as a vocation, rather than merely a career. Tilak had sought to found a political mass movement on Hindu principles – no mean feat, given that Hindu ideology often tended to foster passivity. However, for the time being, Gokhale gave Gandhi sound advice: keep quiet for a year.

Gandhi used his first few years back in India embarking on a side of his work which was not political in the normal sense of the word, but which was to be of great importance in his political work, and to which he would return in the following years when he suffered political set-backs, which would have sent more conventional political figures into retirement.

In *Hind Swaraj* Gandhi had urged a return to Indian roots in the culture of the village. Now he had the chance to start touring a few of India's 700,000 or so villages, and find out just how far short they fell of his ideal. As he travelled around the Bombay Presidency, Burma, Madras, the United Provinces, Delhi and his native Gujarat, the real misery and the practical problems faced by millions of his fellow-Indians was borne in upon him.

Part of Gandhi's response to this was to develop the strand of his work represented by the communities at Phoenix and Tolstoy Farms. He established what he called the Satyagraha Ashram (an ashram being a religious community).

This was to be the experimental foundry of a practicable and distinctively Indian way of life on the small scale. Property in the ashram was to be held in common. But while men and women lived together, sex was frowned upon. Gandhi himself had taken the Hindu vow of celibacy, *brahmacharya*, back in South Africa, and he advocated that the true satyagrahi (follower of satyagraha) should do likewise. Married people,

'. . . can behave as if they were not married . . . If the married couple can think of each

other as brother and sister, they are freed for
universal service . . . Their love becomes
free from impurity of lust and so grows
stronger.'

It was also in the ashram that Gandhi fostered
spinning and weaving as an integral part of
his programme for India. He was convinced
of the practical and spiritual value of weaving
and wearing one's own cloth, or 'khadi'. He
himself would weave each day. It was an aid
to contemplation. But it was also part of an
ideal of Indian society that focused on small-
scale production at village-level. It was an
aspect of the larger idea of Swadeshi, which
includes the notion of 'Buy Indian', but also
involves such moral values as self-reliance.

Gandhi had become well known, thanks to
his South African work – indeed, the British

Gandhi and Mira Bey in London

At the Round Table Conference

awarded him the Kaiser-i-Hind gold medal
in 1915 in recognition of it. The ashram was
supported by wealthy Hindu business men.
But though Gandhi was increasingly revered
by millions of Hindus, for whom already at
this stage in his life he was the 'Mahatma'
('great soul') and an object of veneration, he
was not a conventional Hindu. He set his
face doggedly against Untouchability. Untouchability represented an unpleasant form
of entrenched snobbery, with vile moral and
sanitary side-effects. It meant, for example,
that no caste Hindu would clean a latrine.
This taboo, meant to ensure purity, could
create absolutely repellent conditions which
no one was willing to lift a finger about. At
one meeting of Congress, Gandhi had created a sensation by mopping out one lavatory
himself. It was Ashram policy that everyone
should muck in. Gandhi determined to

welcome Untouchables to the ashram when
suitable candidates could be found. They
eventually came forward in the shape of
Dudabhai and his wife and daughter. Funds
dried up, and dissent broke out within the
ashram, with Kasturbai being among the
doubters. Finally the ashram was saved by
a generous donation from a wealthy Muslim
mill-owner, Ambalal Sarabhai.

Gandhi was searching not just for Home Rule,
but for a way of life that would make it worth
having. As he travelled and tramped the
countryside, he was a living symbol of un-
common potency among the masses. Already
his African exploits had entered folklore, and
wherever he went people would flock, not so
much to hear what he said, as for his *darshan* – a
blessing conferred by the mere sight of a holy
person or object. It was Gandhi's desire to

mobilize the masses according to the discipline of satyagraha to achieve true swaraj. But though he had a hold on the imaginations of millions, controlling them and persuading them to follow his non-violent ideals would always prove much harder.

However, he was emboldened by some early successes. In 1916 at the Congress in Lucknow a sorry-looking figure made his way to Gandhi and announced that he was Rajkumar Shukla, and that he wanted Gandhi to come to where he lived in Champaran. He was persistent; he followed Gandhi right the way back to Ashram. He popped up again in Calcutta with the same request. Gandhi had some difficulty working out exactly what the problem was, but Rajkumar Shukla was insistent on one point: Gandhi was the one to solve it.

Gandhi went to Champaran. He thought he would be there for just a few days, but what he found made him stay much longer. Peasants rented land from landlords, many of them British. Part of their rent was paid by growing indigo, which was then sold for dye, but the development of synthetic dyes and other problems caused by the war were hitting the district hard. The owners tried to convert payment in kind into cash payments. Relations with the Indian tenants had been poor for some time, but this set owners and peasants at loggerheads with each other. Such was the specific problem, embedded in a context of general deprivation, which Gandhi started to investigate.

The local authorities were troubled. Indeed, they tried to arrest Gandhi, though they bungled by doing so illegally. One can see

Gandhi and friend in 1932

Gandhi is arrested in Bombay

why they were so alarmed, only if one grasps the extraordinary atmosphere that Gandhi created. One official reported that the peasants hailed him as

'. . . their liberator, and they credit him with extraordinary powers. He moves about in the villages, asking them to lay their grievances before him, and he is daily transfiguring the imaginations of masses of ignorant men with visions of an early millenium.'

Gandhi won a settlement for the peasants, and also set about tackling problems of education and health in the villages. For him, it was proof that satyagraha could work in India.

One other tactic which Gandhi would use again and again in later years was tried out

in this period. An industrial dispute broke
out between the mill-owners of Ahmedabad
and their workers. Anasuya, the sister of one
such owner, Ambalal Sarabhai (who had
helped to save the Ashram), sided with
the workers and called Gandhi in. Again
Gandhi conducted a painstaking investiga-
tion. In the end he backed the workers, and
sought to promote reconciliation between
the two sides. The means he finally adopted
to promote it was a fast: he would not eat
until a settlement was achieved. Gandhi
later explained that 'the hearts of the mill-
owners were touched'. But the means by
which he had pursued satyagraha were
morally debatable. He had fasted before
within his own communities. The moral
justification for it was that Gandhi was
making personal atonement for his own
shortcomings as a leader, and seeking to

touch the hearts of friends so as to get them to reconsider their position. But in the context of more public conflicts it was a tactic that could smack of moral blackmail.

IN SEARCH OF SWARAJ

To the bafflement of his supporters, but following his own inner logic, Gandhi briefly turned recruiting sergeant for the British in 1918. Though committed to non-violence himself, he still saw Indians as having some responsibilities to the British Empire, including fighting for it. Then his health collapsed, doubtless reflecting the intensity of the inner struggle by which he had arrived at his position. While he lay ill, the war ended.

In the wake of the war, the British government of India assumed special powers under the Rowlatt Act. They proved more trouble than they were worth, for the principal cause of unrest during the period in which they were in force consisted of protests against them. Gandhi identified them as a fit object for large-scale satyagraha. He hit upon the idea of hartal. It was in effect a strike, but normally served as a mark of respect, for instance in time of mourning. It proved effective. However, closer inspection would have revealed that all kinds of local issues and motives contributed to it. How far was Gandhi really in control? The answer came in the form of sickening bouts of violence, especially in the Punjab. Gandhi tried to quell the riots, but was turned back by the authorities. In dismay he announced a personal three-day fast of penance. But

worse was to come. In Amritsar several
Europeans had been assaulted, and some
rioting occurred. A mass meeting was sched-
uled for 13 April in Jallianwala Bagh, a
sizeable, but enclosed space. Some ten thousand attended. Unfortunately, so did the
recently arrived Brigadier-General Regi-
nald Dyer, bringing with him fifty soldiers.
Without warning, they opened fire. In the
ensuing chaos 1,650 rounds were discharged,
killing 379 men, women and children, and
injuring over 1,000 more. Dyer professed
himself well satisfied, and though his career
in the Indian army was at an end, he went
home to comfortable retirement with
£20,000 raised by admirers.

Gandhi cancelled the satyagraha on 18 April.
In his view, both sides had lost control.
However, savage as the British had been

Gandhi in his later years

Arriving in Bombay for Hindu/Muslim talks

on this occasion, the more profound problem for Gandhi was the establishment of genuine Muslim-Hindu solidarity. His career was in many ways dogged by the problem of communal division and violence. Partly with this in mind, he now supported a distinctively Muslim cause: Khilafat. The Sultan of Turkey was, as Caliph, possessed of sacred status under Islam. In particular, he had the sacred duty of guarding pilgrims on the road to Mecca. Unfortunately, on a more earthly level, he had also just been on the losing side in the First World War. The Khilafat movement sought to put pressure on Britain as one of the victors to respect the Sultan's religious function, and leave him enough earthly power to discharge it. As it happened, the cause fell by the wayside when Mustapha Kemal overthrew the Sultanate and established a secular, nationalist Turkey. But meantime Gandhi espoused it, with calls for non-co-operation with the British. Titles and honours were to be renounced and post-holders in official institutions were to walk out.

For Gandhi, the effect was to catapult him to undisputed leadership of Congress. For one thing, crucial figures had recently died: Gokhale in 1915, and B.G. Tilak in 1920. For another, Gandhi commanded a network of political influence like no other.

The British, meanwhile, had shown the paternalistic side of their imperial face in the political reforms of 1919, which established elections, albeit with a limited electorate – about 10 per cent of the adult male population. But late in 1920, Gandhi in

Congress was now making the bold claim that swaraj could be achieved by the end of the following year. The campaign of non-co-operation was carried over into this larger cause. The battle with the imperial authorities was now on – not a battle of violence, but a battle for legitimacy, for the moral authority and prestige on which the British raj depended. The problem for the British would be that Gandhi exercised unique moral force. The problem for Gandhi would be that his satyagraha could all too easily slip beyond his control and into terrorism and communal violence. So it did on this occasion, as murder and mayhem broke out in Bombay and the United Provinces.

The pressure, not just from without, but from his own fierce conscience within, mounted

for Gandhi. It was towards the end of 1921
that he took vows to do half an hour's
spinning a day, and to observe one day's
silence a week. In the wake of news of the
violence in Bombay, the day of silence was
also to be a day of fast. Finally, in response to
the massacre of twenty-two policemen in
Chauri-Chaura (they had been driven into
the Town Hall, which was then burnt down),
Gandhi cancelled satyagraha entirely.

The following month (March 1922) Gandhi
was arrested and sentenced to six years. It was
in some ways a blessing. His periods in prison
were to afford him useful respite from
punishingly hard work. On this occasion,
imprisonment saved him from having to deal
with the after-effects of a policy that had
apparently failed.

49

While in prison he could read, pray and spin. He got through over a hundred books, contemplated the one truth that lies at the heart of different religions, and sat at his spinning-wheel for four hours a day. He was also gravely ill, which precipitated his unconditional release in January 1924.

In his absence, Congress had become divided between those who wished to participate in political structures established under the 1919 reforms and those who would have nothing to do with them. Though an outright split was avoided, partly thanks to Gandhi, the ensuing jostling for position was exactly the kind of politics for which he had no stomach. Instead, under Congress's aegis, he established his own distinct area of activity with the All India Spinners Association, which he hoped would pro-

mote social and economic reconstruction
and regeneration in the pursuit of true
Swadeshi. In the wake of the collapse of
the Khilafat campaign in 1924, communal
tensions between Muslims and Hindus grew
worse, and erupted into violence, to which
Gandhi responded with a three-week fast,
starting on 18 September 1924. This was a
problem to which he was less and less sure he
had an answer, beyond his personal vision
which seemed to reconcile different faiths –
though one should note that in 1926 when
his son, Manilal, expressed a wish to marry a
Muslim, Gandhi opposed him. In conventional politics he kept a low profile for the
next few years. He spent all of 1926 at the
ashram, and was in any case ill again.

It had begun to look as if Gandhi's work had
shifted decisively towards social reform and

During the final hunger strike

Gandhi's few possessions after his death

away from politics. Then suddenly in 1928 it all changed. The 1919 reforms had a ten-year review period built into them. But in 1927 the British Conservative Government, fearing lest they lose the General Election, brought the process forward, and Sir John Simon was dispatched to report on India. On behalf of Congress, Motilal Nehru drew up an alternative 'Nehru' report. At the same time (through most of 1928) a local satyagraha was being organized by Vallabhbhai Patel over the issue of a land revenue assessment in the district of Bardoli. Congress's internal politics suddenly made Gandhi essential, and at that very moment Gandhi received gratifying, necessary evidence that satyagraha was a practical possibility. He was back in the limelight.

The ensuing negotiations were complex – among the things at stake was the possibility of Congress attending a Round Table Conference to be held in London to discuss the possibility of India receiving dominion status. They resulted in Gandhi leading a renewed campaign of non-co-operation. Throughout this phase of his leadership of Congress he was constrained by the internal divisions of the organization, and then, as will be seen, by the communal divisions of India as a whole. This partly accounts for his choice of issue for non-co-operation: defiance of the Salt Tax. It would not divide Congress, nor would it be likely to provoke the British too far, but it would have great symbolic force. Gandhi set off on a pilgrimage with eighty chosen followers – chosen with a view to representing and uniting the different groups in Indian politics. Starting in Ahmedabad, he headed for Dandi on the Bombay coast. People flocked to meet him as he went. All India followed his progress. Day after day he marched, his wiry physique carrying him along mile after mile. It took the best part of a month. At the end of it, Gandhi and his fellows went down to the sea and made salt. The image that emerges of Gandhi is of a fearless, moral pilgrim, a seeker after truth. British rule in India, on the other hand, was made to look silly.

In due course it was back to prison for Gandhi. But civil disobedience continued. In particular, the boycott of imported cloth gained ground. Overall, the movement was of unprecedented scope – a genuine mass movement, though Muslim participation was not so committed. As the Viceroy sought to lay the ground for the forthcoming conference, which would now take place under the auspices of a British Labour

54

Government, he faced the inevitable and negotiated with his prisoner, Gandhi. Irwin was comparatively more sympathetic than many a Viceroy. By the so-called Gandhi-Irwin pact, they arrived at terms that would pacify the country and get Gandhi to the Round Table Conference, though they incurred severe criticism from their respective sides.

By the time of the conference, late in 1931, awkward problems had started to reassert themselves. Though Gandhi went as Congress's sole representative, the problems Congress had had in arriving at a workable position meant that Gandhi's hands were tied. In addition, communal problems were reasserting themselves. There was the possibility of not just the Muslims but also the Untouchables getting their own separate

Lord Mountbatten and Jawaharlal Nehru

Monument to Gandhi in New Delhi

electorates, and the semi-independent Indian Princes were seeking to secure their own interests. With all these problems, never mind the larger problem of negotiating with the British Government, which was now a coalition and had its own unity to safeguard, it was perhaps inevitable that the conference ended in stalemate.

In India, relations between Congress and the government, now headed by Willingdon, a less sympathetic Viceroy, had deteriorated. Gandhi had not been back long before he was returned to prison. From his cell, Gandhi sought to continue his work, showering the ashram with advice and instructions, and trying to heal at least one communal rift by a fast designed to get the Untouchables to abandon the idea of a separate electorate, and to throw in their lot with Congress. The agreement which ended the fast was the occasion for ecstatic scenes between caste Hindus and Untouchables, some of whom were even invited into the temples, from which they were usually barred. But Congress was unhappy to find itself lumbered with the policy of civil disobedience. It wasn't now leading anywhere in the normal political sense. Gandhi, meanwhile, was getting more and more engrossed in social projects conducted with religious devotion, such as a campaign on behalf of Untouchables, or Harijan, Children of God, as Gandhi referred to them. Jawaharlal Nehru, now a leading figure in Congress, and Gandhi's political heir, was not alone when he confided to his diary: 'I am afraid I am drifting further and further away from him mentally, in spite of my strong emotional attachment to him.'

Gandhi continued to pursue civil disobedience. When he was released, notwithstanding Congress's reservations, he set about it on his own account, and was promptly re-arrested. The Viceroy had boxed him into a political corner, and Congress had no wish to join him there. The upshot was a second parting of the ways, closely parallel with the first, ten years earlier. Then, Gandhi had stood aside from the political leadership of Congress to concentrate on the AISA; now he channelled his energy into a similar organization, the All India Village Industries Association. Congress eventually rejoined legal politics by contesting the provincial elections of 1937, which brought it to power in most of India.

MARTYRDOM

Congress's electoral success did not, of course, mean independence. But, for a while, there was some reason to believe that increasing Indian participation in government would lead to full independence in due course. This wasn't an area in which Gandhi's unique skills would be much called for, though he remained an important figure in Congress.

He became increasingly preoccupied with his own spiritual quest, and with life at a new ashram at Sevagram. Though he inspired adoration in others, life in the ashram seems to have been fraught with difficulties. At one crisis, his devoted secretary, Mahadev Desai, laconically summed up his feelings:

'To live with the saints in heaven
   Is a bliss and glory,
But to live with a saint on earth
   Is a different story.'

The world outside had proved less amenable to his vision than he had hoped, though he clung to his religious faith and his work to sustain him.

The outbreak of the Second World War transformed Indian politics. The Viceroy, Lord Linlithgow, brought India into the war without consultation. To Congress,

this high-handedness was confirmation that
the political process in which they had begun
to participate was a sham. As they locked
horns again with the imperial authorities,
Gandhi's kind of leadership was once again
required. Attempts to find terms on which
Congress would support the war effort
foundered, and Gandhi embarked on a
new campaign for the British to 'Quit
India'. He was accordingly arrested in August 1942, and remained interned in the Aga
Khan's palace at Poona until May 1944,
when he was released on medical grounds.
When he was arrested, Kasturbai stood in for
him at a meeting where he was to have
spoken, and so got herself sent to join her
husband. Her own health was failing, and by
February 1944 her condition was grave. In
accordance with her wishes, Harilal, her
eldest son, came to visit her. He staggered

in, drunk. Gandhi and he had fallen out long before, though Gandhi blamed himself for his son going to the bad. Now he was bundled back out of his mother's sick-room. Two days later, she died.

It had become increasingly obvious that, one way or another, the British were bound to leave India – not, perhaps, while Churchill was Prime Minister, but sooner rather than later, all the same. Jawaharlal Nehru became the head of an interim government in September 1944, but the problem of estab-lishing terms for full independence re-mained. Deadlock would finally be broken when the post-war Labour Government sent Lord Mountbatten out in 1947 with the mission of ensuring that he should be the last Viceroy.

The main problem for Congress was to make real its claim to represent all Indians, not just the Hindus. Set against this was the Muslim League, led by the austere M.A. Jinnah. Jinnah and Gandhi had already tried, in vain, to arrive at some *rapprochement*. It was Jinnah's claim to represent all Indian Muslims. The League fell short of this, but fears of Hindu dictatorship after independence went some way to shore up his position. And such fears readily expressed themselves in violence. As independence became more and more likely, communal violence escalated. Jinnah declared a Direct Action Day for 16 August 1944. At the end of it, over 5,000 lay dead.

Mountbatten finally supervised partition: in areas where the Muslims were a majority, they could form their own state. The result consisted of two widely separated parts, Pakistan and East Pakistan (now Bangladesh). The process of separation was tense. Millions migrated in an attempt to end up on the right side of the border. Rioting was rife. Gandhi pitched into the struggle to keep the peace in Bengal.

Twice Gandhi fasted to try to bring his fellow Indians to their senses, in August 1947, when the Calcutta gang-leaders came and wept at his bedside, and for the last time in January 1948. He particularly wanted to secure proper treatment for all the minorities of the new India. He also prompted the new Indian Government to hand over Pakistan's share of government assets. Representatives of all communities, of India and Pakistan, hastened to where he lay, frail and curled in foetal posture, and pledged themselves to peace.

Not everyone was so happy. Extremists on all sides would be harder to tame. Some hard-line Hindus, in particular, considered Gandhi a traitor. On Friday, 30 January, he went as usual to his prayer meeting. Just after five, he set off into the garden, supported by two female relatives. Suddenly a man in khaki pushed through the crowd. He shoved one of Gandhi's supporters away, made a small bow, and let loose three bullets at point-blank range.

That very day, Nehru, leader at last of an independent India, broke the news to the country that 'The light has gone out of our lives and there is darkness everywhere':

'The light has gone out, I said, and yet I was wrong. For the light that shone in this country was no ordinary light. The light that has illumined this country for these many years will illumine this country for many more years, and a thousand years later that light will be seen in this country, and the world will see it and it will give solace to innumerable hearts . . .'

LIFE AND TIMES

Julius Caesar
Hitler
Monet
Van Gogh
Beethoven
Mozart
Mother Teresa
Florence Nightingale
Anne Frank
Napoleon

LIFE AND TIMES

JFK
Martin Luther King
Marco Polo
Christopher Columbus
Stalin
William Shakespeare
Oscar Wilde
Castro
Gandhi
Einstein

FURTHER MINI SERIES
INCLUDE

ILLUSTRATED POETS

Robert Burns
Shakespeare
Oscar Wilde
Emily Dickinson
Christina Rossetti
Shakespeare's Love Sonnets

FURTHER MINI SERIES
INCLUDE

HEROES OF THE WILD WEST

General Custer
Butch Cassidy and the Sundance Kid
Billy the Kid
Annie Oakley
Buffalo Bill
Geronimo
Wyatt Earp
Doc Holliday
Sitting Bull
Jesse James

FURTHER MINI SERIES
INCLUDE

THEY DIED TOO YOUNG

Elvis
James Dean
Buddy Holly
Jimi Hendrix
Sid Vicious
Marc Bolan
Ayrton Senna
Marilyn Monroe
Jim Morrison

THEY DIED TOO YOUNG

Malcolm X
Kurt Cobain
River Phoenix
John Lennon
Glenn Miller
Isadora Duncan
Rudolph Valentino
Freddie Mercury
Bob Marley